About the author

Haythem Bastawy holds a PhD in English and History. He is a Fellow of the British Higher Education Academy and a Fellow of the Royal Anthropological Institute and a former Teaching Fellow in Drama and Postcolonial Literature at the University of Leeds. He received the John Murray Prize for the distinction of his research in 2015 and the SWAPCA Languages and Literatures Award in the US in February 2017 and has published widely on various aspects of English Literature and History. Alongside his publications, he also works on his art and his music. He is in the top 1% of Academia worldwide author ranking. His poetry is inspired by his travels and adventures and is rooted in classical literature.

THE HESIAD III: THE HEROCRACIES

Haythem Bastawy

THE HESIAD III: THE HEROCRACIES

Vanguard Press

Dedication

To my father

Hooda Bastawy

Pharaoh by lineage and descent

Acknowledgements

To Bastet-Sekhmet

The tiger-cat goddess

To whom we owe our surname

(Bastawy: descendant of Bastet-Sekhmet)

Originated in 2890s BCE

In a world that does not exist today.

The Hesiad I, II & III – Prologue

In the beginning there was nothing, and out of nothing came darkness and chaos, and in the chaos the first god came to being. Amun emerged out of darkness like a star newly-formed. All stars are formed the way the first god came to being as a tribute of worship. Amun created the universe, the stars and the planets, and he created a blue planet. For a long time, the blue planet had nothing but water and the water was Amun's mirror. Then one day Amun made a mound above the water and made another god in his image to live on it. He called him Atum. The new god was aware of his being Amun's reflection, but he was also aware of the limitations of his world, his mound and his powers. Atum sought more power and more freedom by multiplying himself. First he created Hathor, who became his consort and the mother goddess. Together they multiplied themselves and created a race of gods and goddesses. But Atum was ambitious: he wanted more power, and more recognition from his father. He settled the Nunn, the chaotic water that surrounded the mound. Then he expanded the mound and made Egypt. And through the heart of Egypt he flushed the Nile out of the Nunn, and on either side of the Nile grew trees and forests and marshes. And in Egypt he made a race of men and women in his and his consort's images.

Amun was impressed as well as overwhelmed by his son's accomplishments. He had created the universe, but his son created a whole other universe on the blue planet, all in his reflection, all in his image, with a race of gods and a race of men who worshipped him every day in the form of the sun disc and called him Amun-Ra. Amun decided to elevate Atum to his magnificence and descend from his throne to live in retirement in his son's creation. He took the guise of a great snake and lived amongst his worshippers. Atum chose his son, Osiris, to take his place on the throne of the blue planet, which was now turning green. Osiris, the green god, honoured his father's work, blessing Egypt with the annual Nile flood, allowing his worshippers to grow crops out of seeds of their choice and for very little toil. Osiris's brother, Seth, grew jealous of his achievements and fancied himself a better ruler. Seth knew he was no match for his brother in power or strength, however. He tricked his brother and mixed potions of sleep into his wine. And in his brother's sleep, Seth tore his limbs and torso into nine pieces. He put each in a box and ascribed a symbol of its shape or significance on the outside of the box with his brother's blood for ink. These are the symbols that Thoth, the moon god, would use to invent writing and gift it to men. Seth sent each of the boxes with one of his servants to be buried under a different tree. Nine trees, all spread out across Egypt. Seth ascended the throne.

Osiris's loyal consort, his queen and goddess of fertility, looked for Osiris's nine sarcophagi, but found nothing. She sought refuge in the marshes, where Amun appeared to her in his snake form. He gifted her with two wings and told her to look under the trees, not in the marshes. Isis flew across all of Egypt for nine years and each year she found a sarcophagus. In the ninth year, she put all of Osiris's parts together and he rose once more. They mated passionately with years of longing. Their son, Horus, was conceived that day. He was born a hawk god, with his mother's wings, with his father's strength, with Amun's golden sun in his skin, and with Atum's ingenuity. Upon seeing his glory, his father elevated him to take his throne and Osiris descended to rule the underworld. He would be remembered and worshipped every spring. The feud was now between Horus and his uncle. Horus challenged Seth to a combat. The combat was not long. Seth was no match for Horus, who stood in the palace peering with an eye of the sun and an eye of the moon. After several strikes, Horus soared up in the air and descended on Seth with his spear. Seth tried to avoid the strike, but Horus came down on him with his hawk-like speed. As Seth shifted himself to avoid the blow, the blade ran through his thigh instead of his chest and went into his groin. In his agony, Seth struck at Horus's face. His sword caught Horus's left eye. This would be the eye that Thoth would use for wisdom before Amun would restore it to Horus. Seth was defeated and banished to the marshes and Horus ascended the throne. His reign was glorious and his worshippers numerous. The Egyptians built temples for him all over Egypt and he blessed Egypt and made it prosper.

One day, Seth sent his consort requesting pardon; he knew he would find mercy in his nephew's heart. Horus was at the peak of his powers, everything was going his way, and he was confident that his uncle was no match for him if they combatted again. He agreed, and Seth returned to the centre of Egypt. Seth was still vengeful, however, and Horus had not accounted for his uncle's treachery. Seth waited until Horus descended into the underworld to visit his father over winter, and locked the golden gates from the outside with Horus's seal. Horus was trapped. He could see but couldn't act, and in the heat of the furnace his wings turned to ashes. Seth took the throne, but he had neither wisdom nor power. The golden age was over. Egypt and Earth would be changed for good. In the third account of the God of Light's diaries, we witness his incarnation which follows on from the second part of the series. The incarnation process allows the god to become human: a god and a man, a mortal and an immortal, a human and a demi-god – rebuilding a new golden age on top of a new mound while navigating his way through various challenges.

The following is some recent notes from the God of Light's diaries:

The Hesiad III: The Herocracies

I spent seven millennia in hell,
And seven millennia dying.
Now my thirst is insatiable.

There is nothing more delicious than sin
And nothing more thrilling than falling,
Beyond east and west, upwards
Is a completely different kind of flying.

28/03/17

They asked me how many languages do you speak
I said several languages and dialects
They said super-talented then
I said a talent wasted, only used for listing elements.

It is shameful this world without worship,
Without a real belief in a god,
Without a worthy enemy to take the blame,
Without a divinity to make a claim for eternity.

23/4/19

Sometimes I wish I could believe in something,
Pray to something, anything,
But all my belief is in myself,
Sometimes this means nothing, sometimes everything.
And I live with the existential crisis
Of an ancient deity who prays to himself.

21/04/19

I don't associate with people for too long,
Sometimes I watch and listen behind a cloak of
invisibility.
And although I don't detest humanity,
Something in me is wary of losing my immortality.

And I take notes many notes
Observing the intertwined diversity.
Even though I'm usually the centre of the action
I tamper my hyperactivity with observations
Just to reflect my universality.

22/04/19

At times I think I want somebody
Who could be part of my bigger plan

But without being a drain.
I guess I need to settle down possibly
But I haven't thought about it seriously yet.
Or maybe I'm not made this way,
Or maybe I haven't met my queen yet,
Yeah, I think that's about it.
Yeah, that's about it.

06/05/19

Now don't envy me.
I've got sons
And I've had many lovers.
But I've never had a family.
And I don't know if I ever will.

7/5/19

But I'm pushing myself too far
All this money and gold
Building an empire, becoming a star.

I've put the new project to rest.
And went on holiday and gave up shaving.
And reflected on the projects that have not progressed.

And the paintings and the drawings,

The sketches and the drafts
That were fed to the god of wrath.

And contemplated a history
That remains alive despite its contradictions
Or previous trajectory.

26/05/19

Yet what would a divinity do
In this paradoxical multiplicity.
Of secularism that is not yet free from monotheism.
Of definitions that borrow from repetitions.
Of atheism that accommodates for regression
In the name of tolerance.
Of categories that create divisions
At the risk of violence.
Of unilateral ways of thinking
That encourage ignorance.

01/07/19

I'm not the last of my line of pharaohs
But none of these languages bears significance,
Sometimes.

Let's reorder the gods

And rearrange the universe.

Let's redefine what's right
And what's wrong.
And put everything in place
And call on a good spirit
To referee this race.

20/07/19

The coroner was wed.
The coroner was lonely.
And all the bodies he met
Were dead and ugly.
So I avoided the coroner completely.

I cancelled the next party
And revisited *The Great Gatsby*.
And the hallway echoed of maths.
After listening to a jazz melody.
And going away and bringing back
New and old records today.

20/7/19

Today I don't feel like talking to people
Which is not me at all.

I just don't know who's false and who's true
Under this theatrical curfew.
Nor who's a friend or who's a foe?
Or which is which?
Or who is who?

Yet I'm an orator not a debater.
I dance first and write later.
Or write first and party later.
And I'm always a lover not a hater.

22/7/19

From city to city flying high
I always say hello.
Sometimes I say goodbye.
Sometimes I just go.

23/7/19

Through a process of explication
And an ongoing journey
From destination to destination to destination
Came a shimmering vision and a revelation
That before the wings could grow back
And the new golden age becomes more stable
There had to be an incarnation after an incarnation.

In the heat of the day
And the luck of the night
The process became complete
In full formation.

24/7/19

Byron shook and twisted his head.
He pondered walking away.
He pondered hitting the road again.
But another decision bothered him instead.

Byron battled with the seas to Greece
Poseidon only let him get as far as Cyprus.
And in Cyprus he learnt some Greek words.

Cypress was great.
Cypress was plentiful.
And its ancient Greek
Was different from the mainland
But still beautiful.

It was Byron's language of Sophocles.
The language of Oedipus.
The language of Aristophanes.
The language of Icarus.

Tonight I'm raising a glass to the infamous ivory
tower.
Here all the books were made.
For a god who looked at the golden dome every hour.

Byron never really died.
He just briefly stumbled
Upon an invisible object
And considered retirement.

He blamed it on a mysterious incident.
He blamed it on the lure of the country.
He blamed it on the Wars of the Roses.
He blamed it on the boom boom.
He blamed it on his sins of the century.

Byron found peace tonight.
Though his decisions were half-made.
But a new light in his chest
Was guiding his formidable fate.
Yorkshire will have to wait then.
Yorkshire will have to wait.

Byron's newly-found peace
Came from understanding that
The heretical god's diary was one of misinterpretation.
And everyone who read it

Added an unfounded meaning for vilification.

Byron raised a toast last night
To the old and the new gods.
He never really had faith in anything
But his faith was in his sons.

7/9/19

Everything was going so well.
Until the horse lost his footing
Until the hunter became game
And all the irrelevant reasons
Were hooked into his name.

He had run out of favours.
He had run out of cocaine.
He had run out of friends.
He had run out of champagne.

He still remained tireless.
He still remained fearless.
His belief in his sons remained.
Even though he was faithless.

His muscles flexed.
His body was ache-less.

He was not out of vision.
But the obstacles seemed endless.

Two months, three weeks and a day ago
Most parties ended.
The wind stopped, the sails dropped
And the sailor was stranded.
In an ocean that was wide and blue
But its supply was limited.
Yet the possibilities were limitless.

The hunter quickly rose to his feet again.
And quickly regained his focus.
He could see far ahead now.
He named his new horse Pegasus.

Byron remembered a time
When he thought he had lost his mind.
And in a very spartan fashion
Attempted to take his life.
But nothing killed Hemingway.

He had come to a new realisation.
After seeking a new confrontation.
That he was dealing with a kind of misunderstanding
Of all his speeches and all his writing.

The poet was once a bard,
And the bard was once an orator.
He did that by day
And in the evening he was a boxer.

9/9/19

Byron was mapping out his decisions
In a geography of mathematical equations.
He was determined to see his stars rise
But needed to make the right calculations.

10/9/19

Half the maths was in his head
Half was on the table.
He could see the circle of life
In a child's fable.

Nietzsche pushed his writing too far one year,
And nearly lost his mind.
Three books in eight months and planning a fourth
Made him go temporarily blind.

The bard was no longer troubled.
The boxer was not looking for a fight.
He could see that something was wrong

Or that something was still right.

I have seen the beautiful nightingale sing
A silent but emphatic song.
The hawk was flying above
Singing an ancient ballad of divine love.

And the hawk was the nightingale.
And the nightingale was the hawk.
And the hawk at times had to keep silent.
And silence was a form of outspeaking at times
When words had already been poignant.

And the love was purely to his offspring.
To his sons he always felt something divine
In autumn and summer. In winter and spring.
At least for those he knew about anyway.

Through them his heart was growing
And learned to encompass the universe
With mutual feeling and understanding,
With faith in his friends too
The old ones and the new
Those who stayed loyal and true.

He was always a man on fire
And out of ashes

He raised an empire.

And through the empire
A river ran wild.
At each of its forests
He made a child.

Jesus accepted an invitation.
He sat at the centre of the table.
The last supper was sweet
But one of his disciples was unstable.

He wore the marks of the cross
On his feet and his wrists
Even after he rose.
Some of his disciples believed him
Some thought it an overdose.

Byron found it funny
How each friend tried to stake a claim
Whether in his writing, in his partying,
In his hunting or in his blame.

12/9/19

A brief conversation with a friend
Made him realise now he must have read the book.

He echoed passages from it nearly word by word.
He read it all and misunderstood.

But this was not very unusual.
Another friend before did the same.
Each trying to be the main character.
False friends who thrive on pretence.
But the main character is in the bard's name.

All will be well
In good time everything will be under his spell.

Look at the sun rising.
Look at the night shining.
There is no mortal death here
Or compromising.

Byron went for a run
Never mind the paparazzi.
Or the vans or cameras following him.

Byron was Jesus
And Jesus was Byron.
At times Zeus too
And at times Poseidon.
They were all different phases of Byron.
Now is a new phase.

13/9/19

Only the brave will however persist.
Only the brave will continue to persevere.
Some friends will rise above the storm.
And in good time, the murky water will clear.

After the incarnation Hercules wondered
What made him temporarily lose his mind.
Was it the ivory towers and feats of glory?
But he had left the past behind.
And was founding a new kingdom in the story.
With new and old allies who would remain loyal
And wouldn't switch sides
During the battle or after the fight.

Hercules was performing the labours
He had to complete.
And redoing the actions
He had to repeat.

And replacing the chalices
That got broken.
And saving the children
While everyone kept talking.

I left Nottingham once.

And I left Sheffield before.
I might have to leave Leeds too
But I'm not yet sure
And Leicester is knocking on the door.

Don't answer!

15/9/19

I have seen the silver nightingale feel
Under the ancient tree of Solomon Steel.
The golden hawk will always be there.
He would neither die nor lose his flare.

19/9/19

Hercules had no regrets,
He was focusing on today
Helping those who couldn't help themselves,
And saving the vulnerable and acting fast.

23/9/19

Hercules's first feat was double,
His second and third were double,
His fourth, fifth and sixth a full circle
And all the rest seven.

And seven was point perfect.

24/7/19

Hercules felt sorry for his friends,
The old and the new ones.
Those who misunderstood him
And listened to a broadcast
That aimed to deconstruct him
And amplified his sins
And glorified his mistakes.

His personality became subject to scrutiny,
His character became the object of mutiny,
His plans were called twisted and bristled
Mapped a continent from its highlands to Brittany.

I have seen the silver nightingale feel
Under the ancient tree of Solomon Steel.
The golden hawk will always be there.
He would neither die nor lose his flare.

25/7/19

One day he stumbled upon a bard
And the bard was carrying a diary
And the diary was of an ancient god

Who used to record his history
Mysteriously,
But not all the time.

Much of the history was good.
Some of it was bad.
And although he did it without explanation
His worshippers came to him in the name of
temptation.

And the bard was the nightingale.
And the nightingale was the hawk.

Hercules did not recognise the story at first.
Unusual times and unusual tides.
And unquenchable thirst.

He could see that what stood against him
Was an amalgamation.
The seer had told him that the tapestry of his destiny
Would come to a halt
Until the god's incarnation.

26/9/19

The bard returned from the underworld
After visiting his father's ghost.

It was something that baffled and amused the nation
More than the apparition had preoccupied the hero
with his visitation.

Call it a séance.
Call it a vision.
Call it an interpretation.
Call it an apparition.
It remained unnamed to the bard
And to the host.

He had his eye on something new,
A new plan twinkled on the horizon.
And although he was keeping it sober.
Sobriety was bound to end with October.

I have seen the silver nightingale's meal
Under the ancient tree of Solomon Steel.
The golden hawk will always be there.
He would neither die nor lose his flare.

4/10/19

Each faction wanted him to join their religion.
Each candidate wanted him to follow their policy.
His enemies said it in the name of learning.
His exes waved with purple hands at his autocracy.

But Hercules was not following.

Ultimately it was a strange affair.
He left a piece of him in every bay
And never went back there.
His positivity was what kept him at bay.

He stood at a new burger shack
And made up his decision
That there was no going back.
The time machine was not fixed.
He was only going ahead now
Even faster than usual
Or initially predicted.

The experiment continued
With its social choreography
And though he took centre-stage
He also watched with everybody
From within and without the cage.
But what's the point?

5/10/19

Hercules stopped looking around.
He now looked ahead.

The tempest will one day subside
But the music will never end.

The fact is he was misrepresented
By foes in the guise of friends.
Their campaign was prejudiced
From the start to suit their ends.

His mistakes were glorified,
His vices were intensified.
And though he aimed to do good,
They called his aims mystified.

11/10/19

The hawkman flew.
The hawkman landed.
He had touched the sun
With his wings unfolded.

24/10/19

Some friends showed up and many hid away
Since the orchestra began to play,
And some turned up in look-alikes
Or just had something to say,
Or drew a new comparison to Hemingway.

27/10/19

Some will attempt to deconstruct his intentions
And plough for references and take them out of
context,
Some may frame his picture with the wrong mention.
But he knew theirs was a testing narrative
Attempting the deconstruction of his dimension.

I have seen the silver nightingale care
Under the ancient tree of Solomon's mare.
The golden hawk will always be there.
He would neither die nor lose his flare.

29/10/19

Hercules drives for inspiration,
Some days for motivation
The age of temptations has intersected,
With the age of provocation.

This morning he woke up
Feeling amazing, mesmerising.
His lustre was new and fresh
And his vibe was rising.
And the breeze carried a hint
Of some mysterious scent

That was enticing.

Hercules came and went
Hunting the deadly scent
With his trident.

8/11/19

December is a good month,
January is better,
To show off the metal
And for life to get sweeter.

For this has been since the summer
A test of endurance.
And everything will be on track
With some perseverance.

And Leeds will once again
Become the God of Light's temple.
The equation is not easy
But working it out is simple.

Hercules was an orator
Sometimes a debater.
He would foretell half the story now,
The other half later.

The remainder however
Will remain greater.

The iron will never sink or rust
The stone will never get mossed
And the wood will never keel;
This ship is bound with steel.

9/11/19

The Pegasus rode at full gallop:
Soon the royalties will multiply.
And the profits from the sales
Will be of endless supply.

The publisher said keep on writing.
In the air there was a whisper,
Good days are beckoning.

10/11/19

Every she was a different she.
And every her was a different her.
There are ones he would not mention
And ones he wouldn't declare.

I have seen the leprous nightingale's meal.

Over the sacred tree of Solomon Steel.
The golden hawk will always be there
He will neither die nor lose his flare.

11/11/19

Hercules was once a singer.
At times a dancer.
Some knew him as a magician.
Some knew him as a politician.
Some as a lover and a romancer.

13/11/19

Hercules was once an orator
At times a debater.
He would write first
And party later.

And party first
And write later.
Between day and night
There was no gater.

Last night was good.
This morning was good.
Tonight he was out for a drink.

Tomorrow too will be good.

14/11/19

They confused the story
With their jealousy.
And looked for a problem
In his policy.

But his positivity
Kept him looking ahead.
And doing well instead.

There was the Hesiad,
And there was the Heresies.
Then the Herocracies and its sequel.
And after that maybe a prequel.

15/11/19

The prequel will have to be future-based,
For much of the earlier adventures had been told.
And much will not be disclosed
And the doors of the primeval times will have to
remain closed.

The previous travels of a forgotten era

And the recent adventures of old.
And all the journalistic reports that haven't been told.
And a future glory that is yet to unfold.

Hercules changed cars often
He changed careers often.
He changed bars often.
He changed jobs often.

He had many partners
But none primary.
He had many plans
And a lot to carry.

And despite all his contradictions
That were the product of his perfections.
He became known as Hector,
The father and protector.
At times as Achilles too
The fast and decisive factor.
And the teacher and the mentor.

And the healer and the doctor.
And the philosopher and predictor.

17/11/19

Wrong theories
Lead to wrong conclusions.
And pre-existing ideas
Would only lead to more confusions.

18/11/19

The steak from the other night was sweet.
It had flavours of Greece and Crete.
But the blood stained the sheet.
The blood stained the sheet.

Change it.

18/11/19

In Birmingham, the fortune-teller
Retold three prophecies
And spread sets of cards on the table
Two were of gold,
And one was Cain would retry to murder Able.
And many were already foretold.

Her Oracle disagreed,
And raised a toast of mead

To Hercules' mighty deed.
The prophecies of gold continued
And Cain disappeared.

It was about time for the Heras to give in.
For even though Hercules changed his way slightly,
He would neither accept their authority
Nor their imposition on his identity.

And would continue this way
Between steak and take away
Or settle on one for good
Or keep going like Hemingway.

I have seen the silver nightingale feel
Under the ancient tree of Solomon Steel.
The golden hawk will always be there.
He would neither die nor lose his flare.

20/11/19

Coeur de Lion kept on living
Beyond the latest dare.
His was le grand nom de Dieu
Et le grand nom de Lumière.

20/11/19

Hercules was always a man on fire.
But whoever was running the other operation
Needed help finding the right interpretation.
But they hear and don't learn.

21/11/19

Hercules raised his axe
Above a multitude of heads.
Before the battle was over
He had won in spite of their tricks.

22/11/19

In Hercules's life,
There were many ages.
All were of confidence.
All were of strengths.
Some were of glamour
Some were of ins.
But this was an age of greatness.
An age of goodness
An age of brilliance.

22/11/19

The age was good
But this was a process of realisation.
Of interpretation
And correction of interpretation.
Or putting on hold the right interpretation
Or letting the interpretations carry on.

And watching and laughing
Or watching and disproving
Or ignoring some interpretations and carrying on.

However Hercules was always a man on fire
But whoever was running the other operation
Needed help finding the right interpretation.
And they hear and don't learn.

25/11/19

And the poetry kept rolling
Beyond all the concepts.

Some see privilege
In what others don't accept.

And some see privilege

In what everyone does accept.

And some speak in rhyme
And some speak in gist.

And Hercules always passes the test.

28/11/19

And some grew more friendly.
And some grew more tempestuous.

And some grew more loving.
And some grew slightly dubious.

And some grew more temptatious.

And some turned ridiculous.
When they learnt that Hercules
Back then was not always virtuous.

30/11/19

And virtue itself was in the classical sense
A way to digress.
And in the modern sense it was
A temporary phase.

Tell me something now
That would impress.

The key to being wise
Was to never get caught
Or get away with vice.

And the key to the best fun
Was to remain pagan.

And the key to staying green
Was plenty of protein.

And the key to over-eagerness
Was to stay keen.

30/11/19

Hercules was asked to discuss things he wouldn't
explain.
And define things beyond definition.
And refer to people he wouldn't remember
And places that had changed beyond recognition
And casual encounters before the current mission.

01/12/19

Hercules won't tell you everything.
There are things he wouldn't explain.
And all the psychoanalysis
Is wasted or in vain.

5/12/19

Hercules lived both
By day and by night.
Sometimes there was no synergy
But the mornings were always bright.

8/12/19

Hercules helped one
After one after one…
And it was always good fun.
But their psychoanalysis was mistaken.

9/12/19

When the tough times had passed.
And the time machine fixed.
Hercules would visit you.
And tell of what happened in the past

And some of what would happen next.

And what ought to have happened.
And what got perplexed
In the process.

12/12/19

Hercules was enjoying a drink in a hostile
environment.
The artificialisation of the club was evident.
But the Heras ought to give up.
Hercules would neither change his ways
Nor would he accept their disenchantment
Nor their attempts to roll back time,
Or their misreading of his rhyme.

13/12/19

Hercules was now a captain
Of a ship with many anchors.
A Jupiter with many moons.

15/12/19

It is only natural
That one does not behave naturally

In an environment that feels artificial
But the spirit will remain actual.

26/12/19

Hercules was aware of some of the Heras'
interventions.
And although he played along sometimes
He would neither change his decisions
Nor their interventions would change his actions.

27/12/19

Qu'est qu'il y a don ton sac?
Qu'est qu'il y a don ton sac?
Il y a beaucoup des cœurs
Et Bezlepkovy

28/12/19

Hercules changed the pace.
Hercules changed the tone.
Still some called him Hughes
Some thought him Crone.

With a heart cast in sand and stone.

But the game was always on
And the season rolled on.

28/12/19

The hotel was full
But the dance floor was empty
The music was on
But the rhythm was Dante.

A new dance floor awaited in town.

28/12/19

The tough times passed
And Hercules went to visit.
Things were still the same.
And after a brief delay
Hercules flew back anyway.

29/12/19

Last night was good but different.
Some questioned the food.
Some loved the accent
But the dance floor was super fluent.
And the numbers were a happy accident.

29/12/19

In Prague, time went back and forth
Sometimes plodding along
Sometimes taking a different course
But Hercules always keeps his source.
The third book in the series was finalised.
The fourth was maybe waiting.
And Hercules was anticipating.

30/12/19

Eight leads to something great.
Five could be a strife.
Two is onto something late.
Four is for the bait.

31/12/19

There was the Hesiad.
Then the Heresies.
And after the Heresies, the Herocracies.
And Hercules was its hero and pinnacle.
And the Hesiad itself was also a trident.
And the bard howled a Herculean howl:
Apollo. Apollo. The Apolliad.

01/01/20

Hercules was chasing a breeze,
A breeze with a silver scent.
A thermal that kept him flying
Upwards and ahead,
No going down
No going back.
The earl is staying.

5/1/19

They tried to remind Hercules
Of things he didn't remember
Of places he wouldn't revisit.
Of actions he wouldn't repeat
While he looked for a new heartbeat.

7/1/19

One could time-travel
Through and through
But there is no rolling back time.
Nor unpicking the ancient rhyme
Nor rewinding to a forgotten destination.
Only the future awaits
With new places, possibilities and occasions.

8/1/19

The trinity followed
Wherever Hercules went.
Sometimes it was a fraternity,
Sometimes it was a trident,
And at times a happy accident.

17/1/19

The sea turned and churned
As Hercules dived in.
And the sand murmured
And chimed in yearning.

The crisp icy water
Enveloped him;
Two opposites burning.

He merged with the sea.
Sea salt frothing around him.
Sea nymphs clinging to his arms.

I have seen the silver nightingale's meal
Under the ancient tree of Solomon Steel.
The golden hawk will always be there.
He would neither die nor lose his flare.

18/1/19

Time was a whirlpool.
Nothing changed anything
Yet the new permanence
Changed something.
And what changed
Was not much.

19/1/20

Hercules flew from country to country
Sometimes in luxury, sometimes rough.
The ports were easy.
But settling down was tough.
And the process was endless
And never enough.

No, nothing seemed ever enough.
But the temporary sanctuaries were a bliss.

20/1/20

The Heras tried oats
And tried porridge.
They tried purple and pink
And tried orange.

Then they tried black
But that was Hercules's drink
Sometimes.

Same old. Same old.
Eavesdroppers misheard and mis-told.
And made him a talisman out of jealousy,
Assuming he didn't have an insurance policy.
And tried to deem his legacy mis-sold.

But the hawk also rises,
Dodging bullets of envy and arrows.
His head is full of surprises.
Striking back at the swarming swallows.

23/7/19

I have seen the silver nightingale feel
Under the ancient tree of Solomon Steel.
The golden hawk will always be there.
He would neither die nor lose his flare.

23/1/20

The travails of repetition
Were part of an intervention.
And the intervention was a recurrent repetition

At times tedious or out of fashion
Or altogether pointless.

But the road ahead was open
With potential fruition.

24/1/20

End of part III

Epilogue to *The Hesiad* Trilogy and preface to the trilogy sequel, *The Apolliad I: Le Chanson de Soleil*

On a very sunny day, a sun beam prismed off a cliff that was at the end of a very long beach. The beam opened up into many colours and glowed off the hot surface of the waves that made their way to the beach playfully in gentle races of foam and froth. At the beach a giant rock turned the waves down one after one. But one of the waves that carried the prism looked so beautiful that the giant rock couldn't turn it down. That was the time when Apollo came into being, out of the union of the rock and the prismed wave. Apollo walked out of his cave, the world in front of him was new. He had the heat of the sun in his face and the hues of the prism in his heart, the gentleness of the waves in his eyes and the strength of the rock in his body. The sea hailed him as a god and baptised his light with its waves and the rock honoured him with its strength, and the sun hallowed his skin with its golden illumination.

As Apollo stood in his full glory and glowed like gold on jet stone, like jet stone on gold, a celestial messenger circled the firmaments, clouding the serene horizon in a spiral of froth as it descended to meet the new god. The Pegasus landed at Apollo's feet, and before it had folded its wings, it delivered a message from Olympus:

> Apollo, You have lived many lives before. As a god and a man. As a man and a god. You had brothers in arms and brothers by blood. You fought many wars and you won many battles. Your enemies feared your might and your friends loved your deeds. In this life your brothers by blood have betrayed you and bit the arms that once saved their lives. Your fellow gods will support you in your upcoming battles. At times you may think that you fight alone, but you will be fighting with the might of all the other gods. The Pegasus will take you now from the rock of Jupiter to the shore. You will live among mortals as a god and a man, a man and a god. The Pegasus will always be there for you. Now ride.

Apollo mounted the Pegasus. The Pegasus ascended the firmaments in a spiral of sea nymphs and froth, and travelled with the god around the world. During the journey, the god saw visions of the lands he had seen before, and the many lives he had lived, and battles he had fought with others, and battles he fought alone, and people he didn't know, and people he had known. At the shore of destiny, Apollo's new life began with new allies and new friends waiting along the journey.